NATURE'S CHILDREN™

VULTURES

by Josh Gregory

Children's Press®

An Imprint of Scholastic Inc.

Content Consultant
Dr. Stephen S. Ditchkoff
Professor of Wildlife Ecology and Management
Auburn University
Auburn, Alabama

Photographs ©: cover: Nature Picture Library/Alamy Images; 1: Hemis/Alamy Images; 2 background, 3 background: Vvoevale/Dreamstime; 2, 3 inset: AaronPattison/Getty Images; 4 background, 5 background: Jan-Dirk Hansen/Shutterstock, Inc.; 5 top: AaronPattison/Getty Images; 5 bottom: imageBroker/Superstock, Inc.; 6, 7: Hemis/Alamy Images; 8: AaronPattison/Getty Images; 11: Mark Jones/Media Bakery; 12: Jan-Dirk Hansen/Shutterstock, Inc.; 14, 15: Iv Nikolny/Shutterstock, Inc.; 16, 17: age fotostock/Superstock, Inc.; 18, 19: Jean Michel Labat/Superstock, Inc.; 20, 21: Altaoosthuizen/Dreamstime; 22, 23: John Alves/Getty Images; 24, 25: Biosphoto/Superstock, Inc.; 26, 27: LWA/Superstock, Inc.; 28, 29: Denis-Huot/Getty Images; 30, 31: Duncan Usher/Superstock, Inc.; 32, 33: Walter Myers/Media Bakery; 34, 35: Harry Eggens/Alamy Images; 36: Greg Forcey/Alamy Images; 38, 39: imageBroker/Superstock, Inc.; 40: Zoological Society of San Diego/Getty Images; 44, 45: Vvoevale/Dreamstime; 46: Hemis/Alamy Images.

Library of Congress Cataloging-in-Publication Data
Gregory, Josh, author.
  Vultures / by Josh Gregory.
    pages cm. — (Nature's children)
  Summary: "This book details the life and habits of vultures"— Provided by publisher.
Includes bibliographical references and index.
  ISBN 978-0-531-22724-4 (library binding) — ISBN 978-0-531-22522-6 (pbk.)
1. Vultures—Juvenile literature. I. Title. II. Series: Nature's children (New York, N.Y.)
  QL696.F32G745 2016
  598.9'2—dc23   2015020045

All rights reserved. Published in 2016 by Children's Press, an imprint of Scholastic Inc.

Printed in China 62
SCHOLASTIC, CHILDREN'S PRESS, and associated logos are trademarks and/or registered trademarks of Scholastic Inc.

1 2 3 4 5 6 7 8 9 10 R 25 24 23 22 21 20 19 18 17 16

Vultures

Class	Aves
Order	Accipitriformes
Families	Accipitridae (Old World) and Cathartidae (New World)
Genera	14 genera (5 New World and 9 Old World)
Species	23 species (7 New World and 16 Old World)
World distribution	New World vultures are found in North, Central, and South America; Old World species live in Africa, Asia, and Europe
Habitat	Deserts, plains, rain forests, mountains, and other woodlands
Distinctive physical characteristics	Large, curved beaks; wingspans ranging up to 10 feet (3 meters) for the largest species; most species have a bald head and neck; coloring varies from species to species
Habits	Spends hours at a time gliding high in the sky while searching for food below; usually reproduces once per year, laying one or two eggs each time; many species mate for life; both parents help care for young; Old World species build nests, while New World species do not
Diet	Eats mainly carrion; some species attack young or injured animals; one species is primarily vegetarian

VULTURES

Contents

CHAPTER 1

Circling the Skies

High above the Andes Mountains of South America, a dark shape glides across the clear blue sky. This enormous bird is an Andean condor. As it flies, it keeps its eyes trained on the ground. After hours of searching, the bird finally spots what it has been looking for. A deer lies on its side in a clearing below.

The bird swoops down and lands next to the deer's body. The deer has been dead for some time, and it has developed a strong odor. Other animals have already eaten some of its meat. However, none of this bothers the condor. It plunges its head into the corpse and begins tearing away chunks of food with its powerful beak.

The Andean condor belongs to a group of birds known as vultures. Feeding primarily on **carrion**, these birds are happy to eat rotting meat and undesirable body parts that other animals avoid.

An Andean condor glides above the mountains of Peru.

Two Types

Vultures are organized into two separate groups called New World vultures and Old World vultures. While there are differences between these two groups, all vulture **species** share some basic traits. All vultures have long, strong beaks with a hooked shape. They also have very wide wingspans. The Andean condor is the largest vulture species. When it spreads its wings, they may reach up to 10 feet (3 meters) from tip to tip. In fact, the overall size of its wings is larger than that of any other bird species.

Not all vultures are quite as huge as the Andean condor. However, even smaller species are larger than most other birds. The Egyptian vulture, one of the smallest vultures, has a wingspan measuring more than 5 feet (1.5 m). This is around three times the length of the bird's body.

Adult male
6 ft. (1.8 m)

Andean condor
10 ft. (3 m) long

Egyptian vulture
5 ft. (1.5 m) long

Though it is small for a vulture, the Egyptian vulture is still a very large bird.

Diverse Appearances

Just as they vary in size, vulture species display a wide range of colors and body shapes. Some are more slender than others, and tail shapes vary. Each vulture species has a unique color pattern, which usually consists of shades of brown, black, and white.

Perhaps the most distinctive characteristic of vultures is a bald head and neck. This trait is shared by all New World vulture species and many Old World species. With no feathers to cover their skin, these vultures look very different from most other birds. Some species even have brightly colored skin on their head and neck. For example, the turkey vulture has a bright red head with a white beak. The king vulture's head and neck are covered in brilliant patches of yellow, orange, blue, purple, and other colors. In addition, many species have folds, ridges, and bumps on their head giving it a textured, uneven appearance.

The king vulture's colorful, bald head immediately sets it apart from other vulture species.

Around the World

Vultures occupy a wide range of habitats all over the world. They are able to survive just about anywhere with open spaces and food for them to eat. They soar above wild savannas, grassy plains, and sandy deserts. They also live in mountains, rain forests, and other woodlands. They can even be seen searching for food above farmland or along busy roads. For the most part, the only places these birds aren't found are Australia and the freezing areas around the North and South Poles. They are also absent from many islands.

Different kinds of vultures are found in different parts of the world. Old World vultures live in Europe, Asia, and Africa. New World species make their homes throughout North, Central, and South America. Within these regions, various species are found in the environments where they are best suited to survive.

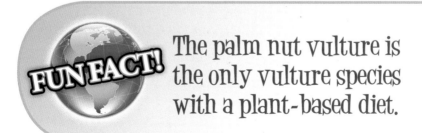

FUN FACT! The palm nut vulture is the only vulture species with a plant-based diet.

Deserts are one of the many environments where vultures live.

CHAPTER 2

Eating What Others Won't

Vultures are mainly scavengers. Unlike predatory species, they do not usually hunt live prey. Instead, they get most of their nutrients from animals that are already dead. Carrion sometimes comes from the remains of a prey animal after a predator has eaten its fill. A vulture's meal can also come from animals that die of sickness or old age. It can even come from animals that are killed by cars. Vultures are not picky eaters. They will feed on any kind of dead animal they find, no matter what it is or if it has started rotting. They even eat garbage and animal feces.

In some cases, certain vulture species will attack live animals. Usually these prey are very weak. Young, sick, or elderly animals can all be targets for a hungry vulture. Some vulture species also attack small animals such as lizards, insects, or even other birds. The Andean condor has been known to attack prey as large as a newborn calf.

Vultures find food where other animals see scraps or garbage.

14

On the Wing

As with most birds, flight is an extremely important part of a vulture's lifestyle. These birds rely on flight to search for food over a wide area. Predatory birds generally rely on fast, agile flying to catch their prey. Because vultures generally do not chase live prey, they are slower and more awkward. But they are built to stay in the air for long periods of time without landing. Because their wings are so large, they do not need to flap very often to stay aloft. Instead, the birds simply glide along on air currents. Under the right conditions, they can spend hours in the sky without ever flapping. This allows them to conserve energy as they travel dozens or even hundreds of miles in search of a meal.

Vultures can also fly at very high altitudes. Even the largest, heaviest species have been spotted as much as 15,000 feet (4,572 m) above the ground. That is higher than a small airplane might fly!

Flying at high altitudes allows vultures to survey
a wide range of territory all at once.

Observing from Above

At such heights, vultures need sharp senses to notice potential meals all the way down on the ground. These birds rely the most on their vision. All vultures have excellent eyesight. Experts believe that some species might even be able to spot a 3-foot (0.9 m) piece of carrion as far as 4 miles (6.4 kilometers) away.

A vulture's other senses are generally not quite as useful in finding something to eat. However, some species, such as the turkey vulture, have a powerful sense of smell. Carrion tends to give off a strong scent as it rots. This can come in handy if the meat is hidden from view, such as in wooded or other areas where it is difficult to see the ground from above. For example, a vulture might sniff out a dead rodent beneath a pile of leaves while flying overhead.

A vulture lands to join in feeding on a large piece of carrion.

Time to Eat

Once one vulture locates something to eat, many other vultures are sure to join the feast. Some species fly in circles above carrion before swooping down to begin eating. Other vultures may notice this behavior and fly over to investigate. Before long, many vultures of various species are likely to gather around the carrion. Different vulture species prefer to eat different parts of a dead animal's body, so there is often food for everyone. However, they still sometimes fight one another for a place at the table.

Some kinds of vultures have unique methods of accessing their favorite parts of a carcass. For example, bearded vultures like to eat bone marrow. This soft material is located inside bones. Bearded vultures access it by dropping the bones onto rocks from high above. The bones crack apart when they hit the ground, allowing the vultures to lick out the marrow. Egyptian vultures sometimes eat bird eggs. They carry rocks into the air and drop them onto the eggs, opening the hard shells.

Bearded vultures eat the meat on the outside of bones as well as the marrow inside.

Useful Features

Vultures are specially equipped to eat things that would make other animals sick or even kill them. By the time a vulture reaches a piece of carrion, the meat might be swarming with harmful **bacteria** or other dangerous substances. None of this bothers the vulture, though. Its remarkable **immune system** can fend off illnesses that rotten food might carry. The bird also has strong chemicals in its stomach that can digest almost anything.

A vulture's bald head and neck is another defense against infection. Vultures often stick their heads inside an animal's corpse as they are eating. If they had feathers on their heads, the feathers would trap blood, bacteria, and bits of food as the birds ate. The vultures would have a hard time keeping those feathers clean. However, bald vultures can simply sit in the sunlight until any mess on their heads dries and falls off.

FUN FACT! A group of vultures can strip a dead animal down to a skeleton in less than an hour.

Even mangled bodies of animals that have been run over by cars can make a tasty meal for a vulture.

Defensive Maneuvers

Vultures do not face many threats from predators. They smell bad, and they are usually covered in bacteria. Most of the time, the only animals that might attack them are other scavengers competing for food. In these cases, vultures do not fight back. They simply fly away and wait for another chance to eat.

Vultures never know when they might find another meal. Because of this, they tend to eat as much as they can whenever food is available. They even have a special pouch called a crop in their throat. The crop can be used to hold additional food to be eaten later. After particularly heavy meals, vultures are sometimes so full that they can't fly right away. However, they are far from defenseless at these times. If an enemy threatens a vulture that has just eaten, the bird vomits on its attacker. The chemicals in a vulture's stomach are so strong that they can burn an enemy. In addition, with its stomach empty, a vulture can escape to the sky.

Other scavengers, such as hyenas, might chase vultures away from carrion.

CHAPTER 3

Social Life

Vultures live together in groups called colonies. Colonies vary a great deal in size, depending on the species. A colony of white-backed vultures might have only 10 to 12 members, while Ruppell's griffons form groups of up to 2,000 birds. At night, colony members gather in trees to roost. Some species move from place to place, while others roost in the same tree every night.

Certain types of vultures are more social than others. In some species, colony members fly near one another as they search for food. In others, the vultures remain separate for most of the day and interact only when roosting. Colony members may communicate with one another in a variety of ways. Old World species can make many different sounds, ranging from low grunts to high-pitched screeches. New World species, on the other hand, rely more on body language to communicate. They do not have voice boxes and can only make hissing sounds.

A colony of vultures might take up an entire tree when it is roosting.

Meeting a Mate

Vultures are very social when it comes time to mate. Male vultures try to impress females by showing off their flying skills. A male might fly in close circles around a female as she glides through the sky. Some species choose a new mate every year. Others pair together for their entire lives.

After mating, vultures find a place to lay their eggs. Old World species use sticks, grass, and other materials to build large nests. These nests may be in trees or other locations that are difficult for predators to reach. Some pairs use the same nest each time they reproduce. New World vultures do not build nests. Instead, they simply hide their eggs in places such as caves or hollow logs.

Most vultures mate once per year and lay one egg at a time. Some smaller species lay two eggs at a time, while huge vultures such as the Andean condor lay one egg every two years.

Old World vultures search out sticks and other construction materials to use for building their nests.

Starting Out Small

After a mother vulture lays her egg, both parents work together to keep it safe and warm. They take turns sitting on the egg so each parent has time to hunt for food. After one to two months, the egg hatches. Like other birds, vultures are born defenseless and unable to fly. A vulture's parents store extra food in their crops and bring it back to the baby. They then **regurgitate** the food for the baby to eat.

For the first two to three months of its life, a baby vulture stays in the nesting area. It relies completely on its parents to bring it food. The baby grows quickly. By the time it is about three to six months old, it is roughly the same size as its parents. At this point, the vulture learns how to fly. It continues to depend on its parents for food, however, until it learns how to scavenge on its own.

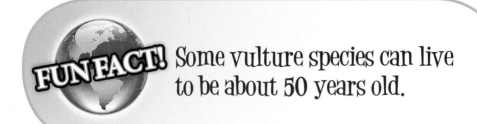

FUN FACT! Some vulture species can live to be about 50 years old.

A vulture parent keeps a watchful eye over its baby.

CHAPTER 4

Family Ties

Birds have been soaring through the skies for about 150 million years. The earliest birds were closely related to land-dwelling dinosaurs. This means that dinosaurs are the **ancestors** of vultures and other birds living today! Scientists made this connection by carefully studying the **fossils** of ancient birds and dinosaurs. They noticed that many dinosaurs became more and more birdlike over time. Eventually, they took flight.

Ancient bird species continued to go through changes. Some gradually developed into new species, while others went **extinct**. These changes resulted in the wide range of bird species we have now. There are 23 different vulture species living today. Seven of them are New World species. The remaining 16 make up the Old World vultures. Though the two groups have a lot in common, they are classified in different **families**. This means Old World and New World vultures are sometimes more closely related to other kinds of birds than they are to each other.

Over time, dinosaurs developed wings and took to the skies.

Hawks and Eagles

Vultures belong to the order Accipitriformes. This group of animals includes hawks, eagles, and several other predatory birds. It is one of the largest categories of birds, with species living all around the world in a variety of habitats.

Like vultures, other Accipitridae generally have strong, curved beaks and dull-colored feathers. They also have a wide-ranging diet consisting mainly of meat. Unlike vultures, however, most species in the order hunt live prey. Some swoop down out of the sky and use their sharp claws to grab unsuspecting fish, small mammals, and other animals. Others snatch insects and other airborne prey mid-flight. Some perch in trees or other hidden locations and wait for prey to pass beneath them. But even some of the strongest hunters in the order snack on carrion from time to time. For example, bald eagles commonly eat pieces of food that vultures have vomited.

Eagles closely resemble many Old World vulture species.

All about Storks

New World vultures have a lot in common with a type of bird called a stork. Like New World vultures, many stork species lack feathers on parts of their head and neck. Some are completely bald, while others have small patches without feathers. Some have colorful skin on their heads.

Another trait storks share with their vulture cousins is the lack of a voice. In addition to hissing and grunting, storks can communicate by clapping their beaks to make loud, rattling sounds.

Almost every part of a stork's body is long and narrow, from its enormous beak and curved neck to its sticklike legs. Like vultures, storks also have long, wide wings they use to glide for long periods of time without flapping.

Storks feed mainly on fish and other **aquatic** animals. A stork's long legs allow it to stand up in shallow water. It reaches down with its lengthy neck and beak to snatch prey swimming nearby.

Some stork species have bald heads that resemble those of New World vultures.

CHAPTER 5

Keeping Vultures Safe

Vultures play a very important role in the environment. They are often described as nature's cleanup crew. These wonderful birds keep dead animals from accumulating in wild habitats. This is an important factor in preventing the spread of illnesses.

Like many animals, vultures must often share their living space with humans. As humans expand their towns, farms, and other settlements, they affect vultures more and more. Because vultures hunt from the skies and eat almost anything, they can adapt easily to some changes to their habitats. For instance, vultures have learned to seek out food near garbage dumps or fly along busy roads to find animals that have been killed by cars. The ability to find food in new places, however, opens up vultures to new dangers. Human activities are causing major problems for some species.

Garbage dumps and landfills are a good source of food for vultures living near human settlements.

Danger Ahead

One problem vultures face is poisonous food. Farmers often spray their crops with chemicals called pesticides. When animals eat the plants, these poisons enter their bodies. The chemicals are transferred to vultures when the birds feed on carrion of infected animals. Even though vultures have strong immune systems, pesticides can make them sick and kill them.

Habitat loss is another problem for some species. With less space to mate and raise young, these vultures are slowly disappearing from the wild. Species such as the California condor and the European black vulture are considered endangered. Conservation groups work to help the birds by raising baby vultures in safe environments. When the vultures are old enough, the people release them into the wild. Such efforts, however, require healthy habitats where the birds can be released. By caring for the environment, we can ensure that vultures continue to soar through the skies.

Conservation workers release a California condor into the wild after it was raised in captivity.

Words to Know

altitudes (AL-ti-toodz) — the height of something above the ground or above sea level

ancestors (AN-ses-turz) — ancient animal species that are related to modern species

aquatic (uh-KWAH-tik) — living or growing in water

bacteria (bak-TEER-ee-uh) — microscopic, single-celled living things that exist everywhere and that can either be useful or harmful

carrion (KAYR-ee-uhn) — flesh of dead animals

conservation (kahn-sur-VAY-shuhn) — the protection of valuable things, especially forests, wildlife, natural resources, or artistic or historic objects

currents (KUR-uhnts) — a continuous movement of air in the same direction

endangered (en-DAYN-jurd) — at risk of becoming extinct, usually because of human activity

extinct (ik-STINGKT) — no longer found alive

families (FAM-uh-leez) — groups of living things that are related to each other

feces (FEE-seez) — solid waste that is released from the body

fossils (FOSS-uhlz) — the hardened remains of prehistoric plants and animals

habitats (HAB-uh-tats) — places where an animal or a plant is usually found immune system (i-MYOON SIS-tuhm) — the system that protects the body against disease and infection

mate (MAYT) — to join together to produce babies

order (OR-dur) — a group of related plants or animals that is bigger than a family but smaller than a class

pesticides (PES-ti-sidez) — chemicals used to kill pests such as insects

predatory (PREH-duh-toh-ree) — living by hunting other animals for food

prey (PRAY) — an animal that's hunted by another animal for food

regurgitate (ri-GUR-ji-tate) — to bring food that has been swallowed back up to the mouth

roost (ROOST) — to settle somewhere to rest or sleep

scavengers (SKAV-uhn-jurz) — animals that feed on carrion and other unwanted materials

species (SPEE-sheez) — one of the groups into which animals and plants of the same genus are divided

Habitat Map

NORTH
AMERICA

SOUTH
AMERICA

PACIFIC
OCEAN

ATLANTIC

Vulture Range

ARCTIC OCEAN

EUROPE

ASIA

AFRICA

PACIFIC OCEAN

OCEAN

INDIAN

OCEAN

AUSTRALIA

Find Out More

Books

Gish, Melissa. *Vultures*. Mankato, MN: Creative Paperbacks, 2013.

Lundgren, Julie K. *Vultures*. Vero Beach, FL: Rourke Publishing, 2010.

Rebman, Renee C. *Vultures*. New York: Marshall Cavendish Benchmark, 2012.

Visit this Scholastic Web site for more information on vultures:
www.factsfornow.scholastic.com
Enter the keyword **Vultures**

Index

Page numbers in *italics* indicate a photograph or map.

About the Author

Josh Gregory is the author of more than 90 books for kids. He has written about everything from animals to technology to history. A graduate of the University of Missouri–Columbia, he currently lives in Portland, Oregon.